CHICHARITO

BY MICHAEL DECKER

WORLD'S **GREATEST** SOCCER PLAYERS

SportsZone

An Imprint of Abdo Publishing
abdobooks.com

abdobooks.com

Published by Abdo Publishing, a division of ABDO, PO Box 398166, Minneapolis, Minnesota 55439.

Printed in China
092019
012020

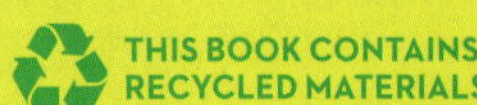

Cover Photo: Marius Becker/picture-alliance/dpa/AP Images
Interior Photos: Federico Gambarini/picture-alliance/dpa/AP Images, 4; Marius Becker/picture-alliance/dpa/AP Images, 7; Mario Castillo/Jam Media/LatinContent Editorial/Getty Images, 8; Victor Decolongon/Getty Images Sport/Getty Images, 11; Claudio Cruz/AP Images, 12; Valery Hache/AFP/Getty Images, 14; Mike Egerton/Press Association/URN:11956847/AP Images, 16; Robyn Beck/AFP/Getty Images, 18–19; Andres Kudacki/AP Images, 20; Giuseppe Maffia/picture-alliance/dpa/AP Images, 22; David Hecker/picture-alliance/dpa/AP Images, 25; Marius Becker/picture-alliance/dpa/AP Images, 26; Charlotte Wilson/Offside/Getty Images, 28–29

Editor: Patrick Donnelly
Series Designer: Craig Hinton

Library of Congress Control Number: 2019941989

Publisher's Cataloging-in-Publication Data

Names: Decker, Michael, author.
Title: Chicharito / by Michael Decker
Description: Minneapolis, Minnesota : Abdo Publishing, 2020 | Series: World's greatest soccer players | Includes online resources and index.
Identifiers: ISBN 9781532190612 (lib. bdg.) | ISBN 9781644943403 (pbk.) | ISBN 9781532176463 (ebook)
Subjects: LCSH: Balcázar, Javier Hernández, 1988- (Chicharito)--Juvenile literature. | West Ham United (Soccer team)--Juvenile literature. | European football--Biography--Juvenile literature. | Soccer players--Biography--Juvenile literature. | Professional athletes--Biography--Juvenile literature.
Classification: DDC 796.3340922--dc23

TABLE OF CONTENTS

CHAPTER
ONE

SCORING WHEN IT COUNTS

Chicharito dribbled ahead quickly. He saw teammate Hirving Lozano sprint past a defender and break free. Chicharito delivered a pass to Lozano. After juking out one defender, Lozano fired a shot into the net.

Chicharito's pass set up Mexico's first goal at the 2018 World Cup in Russia. And it was an important one. The goal put Mexico ahead of Germany 1–0 in the 35th minute. That ended up as the final score. Chicharito—whose given name is Javier Hernández—was playing in his third World Cup, and this might have been his team's biggest win.

Chicharito helped Mexico pull out an upset victory against Germany.

A FAMILY AFFAIR

Chicharito is the third member of his family to represent Mexico at the World Cup. His father, who is also named Javier Hernández, was on the Mexico team that competed on home soil at the 1986 World Cup. His grandfather, Tomás Balcázar, played for the country at the 1954 World Cup.

Germany was the defending champion and a favorite to win it again in 2018.

Mexico returned to action six days later against South Korea. With his team already leading 1–0, Chicharito raced up the field. A teammate passed him the ball just inside the penalty area. Chicharito cut toward the net. He dribbled quickly past a defender. Then he fired the ball off his right foot. His shot rolled past the diving goaltender and into the net.

That goal proved to be important, too, as Mexico won the match 2–1. It was Chicharito's 50th goal with Mexico. No player had ever scored 50 with El Tri, as the Mexican national team is known. He also became the third player to score a goal in three different World Cups for Mexico.

Chicharito scores Mexico's second goal against South Korea.

With his play in Russia, Chicharito showed that he could make an impact with his ability to pass and score whenever he got the opportunity to hit the field. His offensive talent has allowed Chicharito to play at soccer's highest levels all around the world.

Reebok
BIMBO

CHAPTER
TWO

RISING UP THE RANKS

Javier Hernández was born on June 1, 1988, in Guadalajara, Mexico, where his father played professional soccer. At age nine, he joined the club C.D. Guadalajara. Commonly known as Chivas, the club is one of the most successful in Mexico. Chicharito's parents were unsure whether he could become a top soccer player. But by the time he was 15 years old, he had signed a professional contract.

In 2005 Chicharito hoped to make Mexico's team in the Under-17 World Cup. However, the coaches didn't select him, and he had to watch his peers win the title from afar.

Chicharito became known as a consistent goal scorer with Chivas.

Chicharito didn't let that deter him. He resolved to keep fighting for a spot on the team.

BECOMING CHICHARITO

Chicharito's father earned the nickname Chícharo as a child. In Spanish, *chícharo* means "pea." His parents gave him the nickname because he had pea-green eyes. Chícharo kept that nickname throughout his soccer career. Then, Chicharito picked up his nickname, which means "little pea" in Spanish.

In 2005–06, when he was 17 years old, Chicharito played for Chivas Coras, Chivas's lower-level team. He made it up to the club's senior team in 2006. From 2006 to the first half of the 2008 season, Chicharito had one goal in 23 appearances. He felt discouraged and thought about quitting, but his parents convinced him to continue playing.

In 2009 Chicharito began to find his stride. He scored 11 goals in 18 matches, tying him for third place on the

Chicharito was proud to finally get a chance to represent his country in 2010.

OMNILIFE
chivas.mx

Chivas team. He also worked to establish himself on the Mexican national team. In three friendly matches, Chicharito tallied four goals and an assist. One goal came on a header that brought a stadium of 90,000 fans to their feet.

Fans quickly came to love Chicharito's style and appreciate his talent. Chicharito was one of Mexico's top young stars despite standing just 5 feet 9 inches (1.75 m) tall, which is shorter than most other strikers. He used his quickness and ability to get into the right position to make an impact.

During this time, top English team Manchester United began scouting him. Months before Chicharito was set to play for his home country in the 2010 World Cup, Chicharito signed a contract. At age 22, he would become the first Mexican player to play for Manchester United.

Legendary Manchester United manager Sir Alex Ferguson, *right*, welcomed Chicharito to the team in 2010.

14
adidas
14

CHAPTER
THREE

MIXED RESULTS

In his first World Cup in 2010 in South Africa, Chicharito came in as a substitute for Mexico during the group stage. He scored his first goal in a 2–0 victory over France in the second match. Mexico made it to the Round of 16. Chicharito was rated the fastest player in the World Cup. He was tracked on the field at a top speed of 20 miles per hour (32.2 km/h).

Shortly after the World Cup, Chicharito began his career with Manchester United. His manager, Sir Alex Ferguson, thought Chicharito would be a key substitute who would

Chicharito celebrates his first World Cup goal in 2010 against France.

Chicharito made a big splash in his first season with Manchester United.

take some time to get used to the big stage of England's Premier League. But the young Mexican star came on strong right away. Chicharito proved to be a prolific goal scorer in big moments, finding the net four times in Champions League play. In March he scored twice in a match against French club Marseille to lift Manchester United into the Champions League quarterfinals.

By the end of the season, he had tallied 20 goals. His last came against rival Chelsea and gave Manchester United an important win that led to the team capturing the Premier League title.

GOAL POACHER

Chicharito's goal numbers have led some fans to say he's a "goal poacher," or someone who scores goals on rebounds or close-range shots. But Chicharito believes his ability to be at the right spot on the field matters. He puts himself in positions where he can get to the ball and have a chance at a goal.

Chicharito returned to play with Mexico at the 2011 Gold Cup, which is the championship of North America, Central America, and the Caribbean. He opened the tournament with a hat trick and scored seven goals as Mexico won the tournament. The performance earned Chicharito the tournament's most valuable player award.

The next three seasons at Manchester United were a bit of a disappointment for Chicharito. He dealt with injuries and often came in as a substitute, which limited his chances to score. In 2014 Chicharito joined Mexico at the World Cup in Brazil. But he didn't start a single match and finished with just one goal as Mexico bowed out in the Round of 16 once again.

Chicharito went all out to help Mexico win the 2011 Gold Cup.

3
mitre

adidas
Fly
Emirates

After he struggled to break through with Manchester United, the club loaned Chicharito to Spanish superclub Real Madrid on a season-long deal. But after one season in Spain's La Liga—one of the most competitive leagues in the world—the management at Real Madrid elected not to keep Chicharito. Manchester United also decided to let him leave. But a new opportunity was just around the corner for Chicharito. He would find it in yet another European league.

Frustration marked Chicharito's one season with Real Madrid.

LG
adidas
adidas

CHAPTER
FOUR

COMING INTO HIS OWN

In August 2015, Chicharito signed with Bayer Leverkusen, a club in Germany's top league. He quickly returned to form as a crafty scorer. Chicharito netted 26 goals in 40 starts. He was named the league's player of the month five times. He also was named the 2015 CONCACAF Male Player of the Year. That's an annual award given to the top player in North America, Central America, and the Caribbean.

But the next season, Chicharito's scoring struggles returned. He went 15 matches without a goal from mid-October through late January. His inconsistency led

Chicharito rediscovered his scoring touch when he signed with Bayer Leverkusen.

HELPING THOSE IN NEED

In 2012 Chicharito became one of Mexico's ambassadors for the United Nations Children's Fund (UNICEF). He wanted to be a part of the organization to help all kids in Mexico have the opportunity for a better life. In this role, Chicharito often travels home to Mexico to play soccer with kids in his home community or visit students at school.

Leverkusen to let Chicharito leave after two years. He ended up with 39 goals in 76 matches for the German club.

Chicharito returned to England, signing with London's West Ham United prior to the 2017–18 season. He was excited to return to the Premier League after playing in Spain and Germany. He started well, too, scoring four goals in the early part of the season. However, Chicharito suffered a hamstring injury while playing for Mexico. This caused him to miss five Premier League matches for his new club at West Ham.

Injuries made it difficult for Chicharito to get on the field after he signed with West Ham.

WEST HAM UNITED
LONDON
umbro
betway

adidas
KOREA REPUBLIC - MEXICO
23 JUNE 2018
ROSTOV-ON-DON

Around the same time, West Ham brought in a new manager. David Moyes had managed Chicharito at Manchester United when Chicharito struggled to earn playing time. This could have been yet another setback for Chicharito. However, Moyes believed in Chicharito and provided him an opportunity to shine. Chicharito finished the season with eight goals.

Chicharito rejoined El Tri at the 2018 World Cup in Russia. Once again, he helped Mexico advance to the Round of 16. After the big win over Germany, Chicharito scored the eventual game-winning goal as Mexico defeated South Korea 2–1. Mexico eventually lost to Brazil 2–0, but the tournament was considered a success for El Tri.

Following his performance at the World Cup, Chicharito returned for his second season with West Ham. He would

Chicharito was a star for Mexico during the 2018 World Cup.

be playing for a new manager, Manuel Pellegrini, who had plans for Chicharito. He wanted to use the Mexican striker's offensive talent to win games.

Pellegrini's plan worked out well. In 25 appearances during the 2018–19 season, Chicharito tallied seven goals. His highlights included his 50th career Premier League goal, coming in a February match against Fulham. The goal made him the first Mexican player to reach that mark in England.

Transfer rumors swirled around Chicharito during the summer of 2019. He began the season with West Ham and scored a goal in the second week of Premier League play. But Chicharito was soon on his way back to La Liga. In early September, he signed a three-year contract with Sevilla. He hoped to have finally found a long-term home in Spain.

Chicharito scored his 50th career Premier League goal on a header against Fulham in February 2019.

GLOSSARY

ambassador
A representative or messenger.

assist
A pass that leads directly to a goal.

Champions League
An interleague competition for the best teams in Europe.

club
The team a player competes with outside of his or her national team.

contract
An agreement to play for a certain team.

crafty
Clever at achieving one's aims.

dribble
The touches on the ball by a player as it is taken up the field.

favorite
The person or team that is expected to win.

group stage
The part of a soccer tournament when teams are divided into pools of four and play a round-robin to determine who will advance to the next round.

hamstring
A muscle located at the back of the upper leg.

hat trick
Three goals by the same player in one game.

league
A group of teams that participate together in a sport.

professional
A person who gets paid to perform.

scout
To look for talented young players.

striker
A player whose primary responsibility is to create scoring chances and score goals.

MORE INFORMATION

BOOKS

Karpovich, Todd. *Manchester United*. Minneapolis, MN: Abdo Publishing, 2018.

Kortemeier, Todd. *Total Soccer*. Minneapolis, MN: Abdo Publishing, 2017.

Moussavi, Sam. *World Cup Heroes*. Minneapolis, MN: Abdo Publishing, 2019.

ONLINE RESOURCES

To learn more about Chicharito, please visit **abdobooklinks.com** or scan this QR code. These links are routinely monitored and updated to provide the most current information available.

INDEX

ABOUT THE AUTHOR

Originally from a small town in the Upper Peninsula of Michigan, Michael Decker has spent his career as a children's book author, writing about various sports such as soccer. He lives in Laramie, Wyoming, with his wife, three kids, and his dog, Emily.